For Such a Time as This

A Collection of Poems and Proses

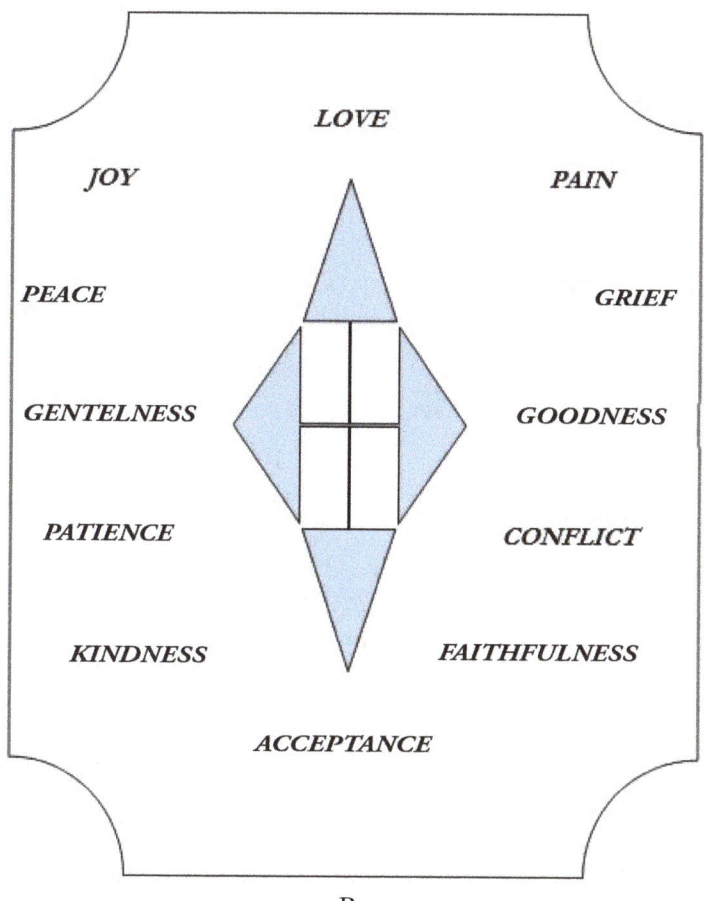

By
Gwendolyn H. Walters

ISBN 978-1-63814-072-6 (Paperback)
ISBN 978-1-63814-073-3 (Digital)

Copyright © 2021 Gwendolyn H. Walters
All rights reserved
First Edition

All rights reserved. No part of this publication may be reproduced, distributed, or transmitted in any form or by any means, including photocopying, recording, or other electronic or mechanical methods without the prior written permission of the publisher. For permission requests, solicit the publisher via the address below.

Covenant Books, Inc.
11661 Hwy 707
Murrells Inlet, SC 29576
www.covenantbooks.com

Contents

Acknowledgments 5

Section One: Love and Faith
    Heart to Heart 9
    A Patchwork of Love 12
    Loving through the Hurt 18

Section Two: Grace and Mercy
    Don't Be Afraid 22
    Right Place—Right Time 24
    Why Pray 28
    The Theology of Problems— A through Z 33

Section Three: Grief, Pain, Conflict, and Compromise
    Advantage Point 38
    Somebody, Nobody, Anybody and Everybody 40
    A Soul in Retraction 43
    A Twinkle in Her Eye 45
    A Twinkle Gone from Her Eyes 47

Acknowledgments

Thank God for my family and friends who listened as I rambled on about the storms of life and encouraged me to live out my faith by putting my emotions to pen and paper. I am forever grateful for their love and long suffering as they endured my boisterous voice while seeing my loving heart.

A heartfelt thanks to Arnis Pape, one of my spiritual leaders, who gave me a venue through my Church congregation to read my poetry. Also, a wholehearted thanks to Karen White, who encouraged me to share my writings and reach out to Covenant Books, Inc. Finally, a special thanks to Leah Holt, the artist who provided the beautiful imageries included in my work.

This book of poems and prose is a culmination of more than ten years of personal reflection and prayers. Surprisingly, as I wrote, I found joy resurface, peace replace pain, and lightness overcome darkness, and I obtained strength to tackle the next raging life storms. I also found immediate relief, renewed spirit, and a reenergized mind while God healed me emotionally, physically, and spiritually. I always felt Jesus's love as I clung to my faith, disavowed the fear, and remembered His death and resurrection for the forgiveness of my sin.

I found comfort and peace in the Holy Spirit's profound conviction of my transformation, resulting in a new perspective while I was guided through a time of disappointment, distress, and discontent. I encourage you to reflect on your own personal walk with Christ and identify your voice, healthy vehicles, and venues to assist you in weathering your storms. I try not to take my blessings for granted. I am persuaded that God blesses us so that we can be a blessing to others. If you ever doubt that, read Esther 4: 1–14.

I'm reminded, "I lift up my eyes to the mountains—where does my help come from? My help comes from the LORD, the Maker of heaven and earth. He will not let your foot slip— He who watches over you and will not slumber; indeed, He who watches over Israel will neither slumber nor sleep" (Psalms 121:1–4).

Section One

Love and Faith

Heart to Heart
A Patchwork of Love
Loving Through the Hurt

Heart to Heart

Heart throbbing, Heartwarming,
and Heart bobbing,

All on the heartrending day,
we first meet.

The heart, so small in stature,
yet essentially enormous in emotions.

It expanded, enlarged, and even exploded;
from the happiness it had found.

Heartache, Heartbreak,
and Heart pain,

All on the day,
it became bittersweet.

We hopelessly walk through life,
breathing in the air.

Knowing without a doubt,
that your mind and body are no longer there.

Heart to Heart, Continued

One event, One evening,
and only One heart,

Torn away and turned back to clay,
once a heart of glistening gold.

Now the heart is grey,
has hardened and turned cold.

A heart can't be so easily won,
after it becomes as hard as stone.

The heart continues,
to beat thousands of times each day.

Pumping hundreds of gallons of blood,
through the vessel each way.

Once red, now black, bruised and bleeds,
and unfortunately keeps others at bay.

I bare my crushed heart,
thinking two hearts could become one.

Can the faint of heart ever
hearten another under the sun?

Only if the hardened heart,
could trust and put faith in the **Son**.

Heart to Heart, Continued

Jesus, all-knowing, knows the condition,
of each and every earthly heart.

He was the very **One** who was there,
in the distinct distance from the very start.

His life was placed on that cruel cross for,
my salvation, now if only I could do my part.

Isn't that really the heart of the matter?
But can that one heart even father?

There's simply no room in a heart,
once it has been sufficiently shattered.

Now, no sunshine, only rainy days,
as all I can hear is *pitter-patter, pitter-patter.*

A Patchwork of Love

I had lost track of time
as I sat for what seemed like two hours
in one of the largest historical
well-known fabric stores in Dayton.

I joyously watched the two,
my daughter and my mother
discuss the design for a wedding dress
that my mother had agreed to create.

The groom asked, the bride-to-be accepted,
the date, the 2:00 p.m. time slot booked,
the exciting announcement made, and
the soon to be wedding was a definite go.

However, none of us knew the journey
that we were about to embark on and definitely
unaware of the ultimate sacrifice that would
eventually be given.

To the right of the store was a wonderful wall
that displayed over two hundred buttons and
included every type imaginable, as well as button
colors, designs, sizes, and shapes.

The adjoining wall held hooks and
eye fastenings, shanks, snaps and studs
that could be used to stitch, glue,
embroider, or applique used for all fabric.

A Patchwork of Love, Continued

To the left of the store flushed to the wall were at least twenty elongated white tables with an abundance of colorful Satin, Silk, Charmeuse, Chiffon, and Lace.

Followed by rows of incredible glossy sheers and lightly woven fabric, a utopia and
perfect playground for any and every seamstress that entered this store.

In the four corners of the building
were rows of slanted stacked two by two
tables aligned with numerous specialty
patterns selections separating each designers.

The store contained Simplicity; the simplest pattern, McCall; a classic pattern, Vogue; a couture pattern, and Butterick; an exquisite stylish pattern for any sizes two to twenty.

I found myself constantly chuckling
as I couldn't take my eyes off
these two patrons, a glowing bride and
grandmother to be, grinning from ear to ear.

A Patchwork of Love, Continued

While my mother smiled and tried not to show her apprehensiveness realizing for the first time as a non-traditional seamstress, she had perhaps reaped more than she could sew.

It's now noon and we needed
to leave the store no later than 2:00 p.m.
to swing by the bridal store on the
other side of town before it closed.

I watched with pierced eyes as each enjoyed their personal honor; one with the privilege
to design and the other, the pleasure
to wear an original custom gown.

Before I could snip in a word,
a salesclerk approached the two of them
and suggested some great seam basting tips
of clipping and cropping the dress sleeves.

Then to trim and tuck the train, making it easier to dart forward, as they face the challenge with greater ease, giving more time to focus on the gown's waistline, and skirt.

It was recommended that the white,
satiny fabric be cross-stitched in two places, and hand stitch to bind the lower part of the gown's bodice to the top of the gown.

A Patchwork of Love, Continued

This technique would help to compliment
my daughter's curvy, full-bosom physique,
and permit room to make any incisions in the
event of weight loss or weight gain.

Gathering my thoughts, I realized that tomorrow
I had a daunting two hundred-mile stretch South
to my home town, Louisville, leaving my mother
to yes, press on alone.

The next day trip to Dayton would be my
daughter's first fitting to do all the basing,
draping, sizing, and notching out as much time
as possible for my mother as needed.

That night, my mother, working with pen and
paper managed to sculpture twenty pieces
from the four patterns, an entirely new scalloped,
shoulder-sloped neckline design.

The next morning, with eyes crossed and glazed
over she presented to us a unique
design and asked my daughter's opinion of the
new outline of silk silhouette and motifs.

My daughter, sitting at dining room table, picked
up a pencil within twenty minutes had etched,
erased, and edited the design then slid the sketch
towards my mother for her review.

A Patchwork of Love, Continued

With raised eyebrows, she smiled, and stared at the sketch for two minutes, then said, "I loved it, it's A Patchwork of Love." It was
the perfect bodice for her granddaughter.

Thankfully, that daunting day arrived when eight bridesmaids, eight ushers walked two by two down the aisles, each taking their place and boldly smiling at the front of the Church.

The bridegroom looked anxiously, awaiting for his sensational, stunning bride-to-be to
saunter and sashay down the aisles in her exquisite one-of-a-kind glowing gown.

The news had quickly spread throughout our family and friends of the designers of the wedding gown, but the guest were still in shock and awe of the amazingly crafted gown.

My daughter strolled past the pews as the gown's beauty illuminated from the soft, patchy, white lights as all eyes were fastened on her while the groom awaited his new bride.

The receiving line at the Church was full of well-wishers, for the two newlyweds, but it was at the reception where she was hemmed in by those who gathered to see the gown.

A Patchwork of Love, Continued

The truth about the gown's cost would secretly remain woven within two people.
As for as the gown's value, well my daughter said, "It's a one-in-a-million-dollar gown."

The wedding gown was the last thing that my mother would ever sew, as she was struck down with cancer two months after the wedding and died seven months later.

The million-dollar dress hangs inside out in my daughter's closet and the two of us await that day when another granddaughter will saunter down the aisle in this priceless gown.

Of course, this will undoubtedly bring back loving memories of August 15, 1993, when she struts down the aisle, and now you know why it's called, "A Patchwork of Love."

Loving through the Hurt

If only it was as easy to love through the hurt as it
is to fall deeply, romantically in love.
What a fascinating thought,
wouldn't you agree?

Yet, not easily applied when
you have been hurt you see.
Sometimes the hurt is met with
regret, remorse, and repentance.

Other times it is surrounded
with a smug smile or piercing eyes,
backed with harsh words sharper
than a two-edged sword.

It's hard to hide the hurt in one's heart,
as it bleeds through, wouldn't you agree?
Even in their voice, you can easily detect the drip,
dribble and tone of disappointment.

Our natural instinct is to chastise, criticize or
reprove, rebuke and evoke punishment.
All the while fighting back and suppressing
emotions designed to soften the demeanor.

What a funny thing, wouldn't you agree?
Oh, how differently we see others when we aren't
in their shoes, but instead step in
and become the judge, jury and mean.

Loving through the Hurt, Continued

Once a caring, concerned, and cheerful person
full of love, mercy, and plenty of grace now
consumed with fire, rage, and a desire to inflict
pain at any time and keep up the pace.

Really, our hearts should be saying, no, no, please
stop the pain, wouldn't you agree?
But our devilish demonstrative mind tells us yes,
yes, keep applying the pressure you see.

Even when there's a softening of our hearts,
be assured it won't last long if Satan has a say.
With that silent scolding voice calling out to
administer more punishment, then says, yea.

After all, eliminating punishment is
not an option, wouldn't you agree?
They're guilty, not innocent, and there's no
goodness to be found in letting them plea.

Wow, how soon we forget that at one time we
were in their spot and tried to flee.
We wishfully wondered when it is us why, oh
why, can't others forgive and just let them be.

Loving through the Hurt, Continued

Isn't that exactly what Christ did for you and me,
on the cross wouldn't you agree?
Instead of punishing us the author and finisher
took our path how can you disagree.

He extended love over the law, mercy over
personal malice, and grace over gracelessness.
We must recognize His goodness, not reject this,
which would be viewed as faithlessness.

What a beautiful thought, wouldn't you agree
how His unselfishness gave birth to the Spirit.
It comes to you and me, giving us absolute
freedom, not forcing himself or even prohibit.

Now we are able to live by a higher standard and
guided by a moral compass you see.
Loving through the Hurt and showing what it
means to be a child of God is a daily decree.

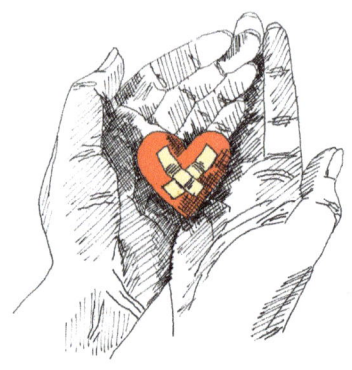

Section Two

Grace and Mercy

Don't be Afraid
Right Place—Right Time
Why Pray?
The Theology of
Problems—A through Z

Don't Be Afraid

In the twilight of the night I saw two angels
One was the light and the other, the night
"Don't be afraid," they said.
"Why are you here?" I said.
"For the lightness," said the light.
"For the darkness," said the night.

In the break of the day, I saw two lamps
One was bright and the other dim
"Don't be afraid," they said.
"Why are you here?" I said.
"To illuminate your path," said the bright.
"To soothe your day," said the dim.

In the midst of the day
I saw a dove and a burning bush
One was flying and the other on fire
"Don't be afraid," they said.
"Why are you here?" I said.
"With a message," said the flying.
"To warm your day," said the fire.

At the dust of the day I saw a fountain
of water and felt a rushing wind
The water was cool blue, the other a cold chill
"Don't be afraid," they said.
"Why are you here?" I said.
"To quench your thirst," said the water.
"To breathe new life," said the wind.

Don't Be Afraid, Continued

At the end of the day I saw the Trinity
"Don't be afraid," they said.
"Why are you here?" I said.
"To strengthen you," said the Father.
"To encourage you," said the Son.
"To comfort you," said the Holy Spirit.
"To provide unconditional love,"
said All Three.

Right Place—Right Time

Have you ever looked back
In your adolescent years
In your early youth years
In your middle and/or old age years?

Have you ever asked yourself
Why am I here?
Who am I supposed to be?
What is my purpose in life?

Have there been times in your life
When God seemed absent
When God appeared silent
When God seemed distant

Have there been times when you felt that
God's Hands were not in motion
God's Voice couldn't be heard
God's Plans seemed to have vanished

Have you considered that God has placed you
In the right place
In the right position
In the right time for "Such a Time as This?"

So, I encourage you, even when you
Can't see God
Can't feel God or
Can't hear God

Right Place—Right Time, Continued

Rest assured
His timing is
Always perfect and to
Remain focus on…

God's Unabating Power
God's Unyielding Promises
God's Unwavering Protection and
God's Undiscriminating Provisions

Do you remember the story of Mordecai
And his cousin, Queen Esther,
Whose bravery saved the life of a King
And the Jews from an eminent destruction?

It was an evil and conniving Haman,
An Agagite who hated the Jews,
But in the end Esther's humility
Prevailed over Haman's vanity.

Do you recall the story of the wealthy daughter
Of Pharaoh and Baby Moses?
A Hebrew baby boy that floated down the Nile
River in a basket made of "Bulrushes?"

This powerful woman took pity on the child
And rescued him, whereby he later became
Educated, cultivated and the deliverer of the
Israelites from a life of slavery in Egypt?

Right Place—Right Time, Continued

What about the story of the Harlot Rahab
From the Book of Joshua, where a Canaanite
Woman ignored the government's edict and
Saved the lives of two spies sent by Joshua.

She hid them under bundles of flax drying on
Her roof, resulting in her and the life of her
Family being spared when Jericho was destroyed
By the men from Joshua's army.

How about the story of Ruth the Moabite
And Boaz an Elimelek, an honorable man
Who allowed a foreign daughter-in-law to shelter
And glean in his bountiful fields?

Without limitation or retribution,
She enjoyed refuge under his redeeming wings
And later a union of two was formed,
Which lead to a miraculous First Born?

Who could ever forget the amazing story of Mary,
The Virgin and her Son Jesus.
A young woman from the House of David who
Had a wondrous visit by an Archangel.

Gabriel came with a miraculous message that
She had found favor with God and that she
Would bore a Male Child and He would be
Called wonderful, Lord, Messiah, and King.

Right Place—Right Time, Continued

It was because of Faith, Love, and Trust in
God of each of these characters mentioned that
There was an inexplicable blessing and "Reversal
Of Fate" in these individual's life.

Thereby allowing many souls to be spared
And precious lives to be saved, therein giving us
The foundation of an eternal life when our Lord,
Redeemer, and Savior gave up His.

Why Pray

(Inspired by the sermon "God Listens" by Arnis Pape, Westport Road Church of Christ)

A walk-through life at any age,
time, or season can be challenging,
and yet that difficult time can produce
an awesome blessing from God.

Some might even say that it builds character,
others feel it develops humility,
while many have sensed it's none of the above
because it created absolute hostility.

There are so many questions to the whys of life
that can only be answered by
the Holy One who knows all, see's all,
feels all and is conceptually our all.

When was the last time you called out,
or asked for a helping hand?
Was it when you faced a crisis,
failed a test, or fought back a tear?

Was it when you risked it all,
succumbed to temptation,
ran afoul or fell flat on your face
in horrible dishonor and disgrace?

Why Pray, Continued

What was the first thing
you did or the first person you called?
Perhaps a loving family member or a supportive
friend, it could have been.

But, more than likely
it wasn't that One that's a
member of that Royal Family
and known as a friend to the friendless.

So, I encourage you the next time you are down
in the dumps, defeated by bad luck,
disappointed, depressed, or despondent by your
life or the events of this world, Pray!

The Word advises, admonishes and advocates
that it's less about us, stop all the fuss,
you must look outwardly and not inwardly to the
One who extends into eternity.

Remember that we are too blessed, beyond our
limited comprehension, to be stressed.
A price paid, a path paved, and a war waged for
our sins so we could be eternally saved.

A Prayer is more than a conversation,
it engages all of our five senses:
We ask with our hearts, a nonverbal request
involving more than the moving our mouth.

Why Pray, Continued

We seek with our souls, a conscientious search deeper than the motion in our eyes.
We knock at the door of grace, a maneuver more than the movement of our hands.

We listen for the reply, an active act of intense waves flowing through the canals of our ears.
We inhale the sweet aroma of thanksgiving and enjoy the smell of peace in our nostrils.

Praying is entering an atmospherical, empirical, spherical, and spiritual place
where you meet one on one with our Lord and Savior and experience His amazing grace.

It doesn't require a prostrate position to enter this private or public special space, but simply a bold attitude, a humble heart, an open mind, and a gracious and submissive face.

It's irrelevant about which room you select in our house, but more about our honest case
laid out before the Lord, in our pain; then being patient as He responds at His own pace.

Why Pray, Continued

I've Prayed in all the rooms in my house, from the quietness of the bathroom, the openness of my living room, only to find that the best room was giving up my headroom.

I've cried out while silently riding in my car, sprawled out in seclusion on my closet floor, while strolling around my neighborhood,
but finally come to a statement of realization.

It wasn't about saying the right thing,
but sharing each and everything and making sure to include any, and all things whether it was scary, favorable or unfavorable things.

You see, there's absolutely nothing
that can't be shared in prayer as long as
it's from the heart, it's authentic, and it's the real deal, real thing and the worrying thing.

Praying, an emotional, physical, and spiritual awakening encompassing a symphony of words received by our Lord as an array of attributes presented in a fascinating harmony.

Jonah will tell you to speak from
that special place in the pit of your soul
since there's nothing too deep, too hard,
too bad, too tough or too old to share.

Why Pray, Continued

There's nowhere we can run, hide, or escape
that Jesus isn't already there because everywhere,
anywhere and somewhere
He abides, resides and presides.

We find Him somewhere
along that wary way when we
genuinely, honestly, and sincerely
ask and let go of our sinful mortal pride.

The heart of the matter is that Jesus
loves us categorically, completely without
conditions and there is emphatically nothing we
can do that will make Him love us less.

We are worth saving, a decision made eons ago
before He faced that cruel, calculated cross,
which gave Him the authority to defeat death, a
feat that none of us could face.

A dedicated, defensible, dependable and
reliable redeemer He was on that day.
So why not today, why not now,
why not submit yourself and pray!

The Theology of Problems A through Z

(Inspired by the Sermon,
"Problems" by Bryan Jones,
Newburg Church of Christ)

God uses problems not to **A**nnoy us;
but to remind us we are His **A**nointed one.

God uses problems not to **B**rush us aside;
but to **B**ring us closer to Him.

God uses problems not to **C**ontrol our life;
but to bring **C**omfort to us internally.

God uses problems not to **D**emand loyalty;
but to **D**isagree with us when we are wrong.

God uses problems not to show how **E**vil
we are; but to show His *E*verlasting love.

God uses problems not, so we get **F**ixated on
serving; but to shift **F**ocus to our soul's salvation.

God uses problems not to **G**uilt
us into submission; but to gently
Guide us into obedience.

God uses problems not to **H**arm us;
but to **H**umble us.

The Theology of Problems, Continued

God uses problems not to **I**rritate us;
but to **I**nitiate His will for us.

God uses problems not to **J**udge us;
but to remind us of **J**esus's
Justification for our lives.

God uses problems not to **K**nock us down;
but to show the benefit of
being on bended **K**nees.

God uses problems not to **L**augh in our face;
but to **L**ift us up above the fray.

God uses problems not to make our lives
Miserable; but to show His **M**onumental **M**ercy.

God uses problems not to **N**eglect us;
but to show us the **N**ewness of life in Christ.

God uses problems not to **O**rchestrate our lives;
but help us **O**vercome the daily temptations.

God uses problems not to **P**enalize us; but to
demonstrate His **P**rovidence and show how
Proactive He is behind the scenes in our lives.

The Theology of Problems, Continued

God uses problems not to sink us in **Q**uicksand;
but to **Q**uarantine us from the untruth.

God uses problems not to **R**eject us;
but to **R**edirect and **R**eveal a more
Resounding way of life.

God uses problems not to have us **S**ettle
for a quick microwaveable **S**olution; but
to **S**how us a **S**low, **S**immered Crockpot
resolution to **S**teady our path.

God uses problems not to **T**empt us;
but to allow us to be **T**emporarily
Tested then, **T**emper us.

God uses problems not to **U**ndermine
the decisions we make; but to
encourage us to **U**tilize our gifts.

God uses problems not to expose **V**anity in
our lives; but to enhance the **V**irtues needed.

God uses problems not to **W**eigh us down;
but assist us in **W**eathering the storms.

The Theology of Problems, Continued

God uses problems not so we will become
Xenophobic and hide from the truth;
but so, we will have a **X**ylan coating
preventing the erosion of the truth.

God uses problems not to have us **Y**ell about
the injustice in our life; but so, we can **Y**ield
to His word and **Y**earn for justice in all lives.

God uses problems not to **Z**ap us
when mistakes are made; but to show
the **Z**eal of His forgiveness.

Section Three

Grief, Pain, Conflict, and Compromise

Advantage Point
Somebody, Nobody,
Anybody and Everybody
A Soul in Retraction
A Twinkle in Her Eyes
A Twinkle Gone
from Her Eyes

Advantage Point

Two different individuals
Two separate souls
    One quirky and eccentric
    One with its own idiosyncrasies.

Two distinct sets of eyes
Two unique advantage points
    One enjoys repetition
    One prefers unrepeatability.

Two styles of learning
Two evolved communication skills
    One uses a familiar, practical approach
    One presents a picturesque delivery.

Two ways of hearing,
Two dueling channels of listening
    One open and in a class of its own
    One closed and chooses solitary.

Two uncommon voices in the distance
Two singular tones so unrelated
    One seeks rare solutions
    One selects traditional resolutions.

Two spirits passing in the night
Two entities wanting to appear strong
    One focused more on being right
    One concerned with not being wrong.

Advantage Point, Continued

Two opposite sides taking a stand
Two trying to recall what's so grand.
    One seeks the upper hand
    One sticks its head in the sand.

Two individuals who seem to belong
Two faces not the inevitable to prolong
    One praying and singing a song
    One reflecting and being headstrong.

Two lonely hearts who can't feel the other
Two wary souls longing for another
    One waiting to make their point
    One wanting not to disappoint

Two finally deciding to withdraw their hand
Two praying that the other has a better plan.
    One weighing who was right
    One wondering was it worth the fight!

Somebody, Nobody, Anybody and Everybody

Somebody
has been hurt, which created pain.
Nobody
wants to acknowledge it or accept the blame.
Anybody
could who most likely have taken aim.
Everybody
claims innocence without offering up a name.

Somebody
says hurt reminds them of love in a way.
Nobody
would ever know if you kept others at bay.
Anybody
experiencing hurt recalls, it hasn't faded away.
Everybody
has a story to tell about the heart awful day.

Somebody
gave an equation that one and one makes two.
Nobody
can gather a divide heart once it's broken into.
Anybody
who looks to Jesus knows it turns from you.
Everybody
knows it's hard when it leaves one so blue.

Somebody, Nobody, Anybody and Everybody, Continued

Somebody
said that God's love is unconditional.
Nobody
should ever try to make it conditional.
Anybody
not knowing better cries out, "it's positional."
Everybody
should know God's love is simply relational.

Somebody,
tried broke love into the lowest denominator.
Nobody
can be lose the love of our maker and creator.
Anybody
unaware is a lost soul, ask your neighbor.
Everybody
can read about depths of love by an author.

Somebody
rebounds from hurt in two-day recovery time.
Nobody
will admit if they need a little more time.
Anybody
can survive hurt, with Christ in due time.
Everybody
will eventually discover that love is full time.

Somebody, Nobody, Anybody and Everybody, Continued

Somebody
failed then lead with malice and viciousness.
Nobody
can find love while holding their bitterness.
Anybody
accepting Jesus is letting go of fearfulness.
Everybody
the key to removing hurt is in forgiveness.

Somebody
said God's love and wisdom is unforgettable.
Nobody
knows when God's will shall be enforceable.
Anybody
who tells you differently isn't at all believable.
Everybody
who trust in His Word will be transformable.

A Soul in Retraction

I could feel in my heart
the hurt, the hesitancy,
as my eyes rolled back into my head.

I had withdrawn my hand, backed away from the
Word, my head held low, humiliated,
once again hemming myself in a corner.

Too late to recant, renounce, revoke, or rescind.
There was no backtracking, backing out of it the
damage was done.

I had fallen back into my old ways.
But thanks to the God Heads that
the outcome wasn't the end of my story.

It was just the beginning since way back,
at the time of Creation, a final plan was
being reviewed and soon would be revealed.

A Soul in Retraction, Continued

It had been decided way back then that
Jesus would be the chosen One to become human
and travel backwards to earth.

To turn around an evil act
that turn about my soul,
which was lost and needed finding.

So as a result of His inverted love for me in the end, what appeared to be a look behind was actually a view from the beginning.

A rearward preparations made for a remarkable redemption, of a soul salvation that only He could have turned around.

A Twinkle in Her Eye

A thought, an act, an afterthought
not quite yet planned.
We all started this way,
somehow, sometime, somewhere.

Love lost, lust wasted, love taken,
love given, or even forgiven.
Then something takes place and
the unexpected happens.

One day we met, I'm attached
and living a luxurious life.
As I rest and develop
in a soft, warm womb.

Three months, I nourished,
I grew, I floated, and I thrived.
On the various nutrients
contained my tiny little yolk sac.

Six months, I'm excited,
I'm energized and eager to go.
Wow, come eyes, come nose,
come ears and come toes.

A Twinkle in Her Eye, Continued

Nine months, I'm anxious,
I'm antsy and I'm also afraid.
Of leaving the only home that
I have known ever since conception.

No months, left and
So, it won't be very long,
I feel the warmth, and hear a
lovely voice crying out my name.

Okay, okay, now I'm ready,
I'm ready, I'm ready to go.
I'm so tired of being shook
upside down, over and over you know.

Wow! I think it's happening,
the journey is over; finally,
right side up and all aglow
As I hear my wonderful mother say.

Praises to the Almighty God,
it was worth the wait,
for my adorable, beautiful,
lovable, and remarkable baby girl.

A Twinkle Gone from Her Eyes

Day one, an unexpected phone call, I can't believe
it and I gasp for air.
My hand, my head, and my body shaking in
despair, it just isn't fair.

Day two, I go limp, I can't breathe,
I can't think, I can't see.
The burning love in my heart turns
lukewarm then cold as ice, it can't be.

One month still numb, even the
warm blood can't penetrate.
My lonely, cold, and empty heart,
oh wow, I just can't think straight.

Six months, I'm desperately trying
to move on with a smile here and there.
But it's not working, my life will never be what it
was when she was here.

Nine months, I'm so exhausted and
so tired of pretending that it's getting better.
It's not and I'm stuck and still spend several days
sad and sorrowful, I must find shelter.

A Twinkle Gone from Her Eyes, Continued

Twelve months, I can fool some
family and friends some of the time.
But I can't fool myself or the Lord
not at all now that I have lost what's mine.

Every month I'm relying on God's
merciful love and His amazing grace.
I know that my loved one is in a much better, yes
that wonderful heavenly place.

Every day, it's my faith in Christ that strengthens
me and allows me to rise this day.
Perhaps this day will bring that which has alluded
me while I have kept others at bay.

Every night I pray a prayer of thanksgiving
realizing it is you Lord who gets me up.
I'm also grateful for my family and friends
knowing each us will drink from this cup.

Tomorrow, I'll look forward to rising
the next day with peace and joy in my heart.
As the two sets of footprints in that sand
have now turned into once we were a part.

A Twinkle Gone from Her Eyes, Continued

It's the Lord that carries her soul and
caresses me as He completely understands.
Every year on her birthday I remember
that so unexpected phone call still stands.

When the love of my heart left me alone,
she was definitely my all and all.
She has returned back to our Savior and Creator
and never ever will she fall.

A twinkle that started long ago in her eye,
has shifted to me as the years went by.
As I think of her often, I soon realized the
twinkle has gone from my eyes as I sigh.

I continue to trust in God who knows all,
He never gives more than we can handle.
With time, my footsteps will again appear in
the sand as I strap on my smile and my sandal.

I look forward to the day when I see her face in that beautiful place that has been prepared. But until that day, my heart will have to carry what my mind can't until we are again paired.

> "But who knows, you may have been put in a place for such a time as this."
> —Esther 4:14

Have you ever wondered why we have to suffer? It has been said that life isn't always a walk through a rose garden. But at times, a grueling stroll through the storms of life leave some devastated and others constantly jumped over hurdles while striving for the finished line.

This book, a culmination of years of personal self-reflections of actions, emotions, motives, and regrets is how the author responded when she felt an exhilarating mountain top experience, only to be thrown off the cliff to a strenuous dark valley encounter. God represents unconditional love and never tempt us, but He does allow trials and tribulations to take place in our life to help shape and mold us into the person He intended us to be.

For Such a Time As This will open our eyes to Satan's tactics, encourage you through personal life storms, and remind us of the importance of continuing to have faith, give praises, offer up prayers and trust God, the author and finisher of our life.

About the Author

Gwendolyn H. Walters is a retired banker and educator who holds a Master of Arts and Bachelor of Science Degrees from the University of Louisville. She was also an adjunct faculty member at the University of Louisville, Jefferson Community College, and the American Bankers Association.

She is an active and devoted member of the Westport Road Church of Christ in Louisville, Kentucky. She currently writes material and teaches Women Bible Classes. Although she has written several manuscripts, this is her first publication.

After the author's retirement, something happened that wasn't planned. She found her voice and accepted the fact that perhaps she had come to a position in her life for such a time as this. From a young age, she enjoyed singing; however, this voice was not to be found in music, but in the written word. Knowing that Father knows best, her voice was enhanced by talking less, listening more to the Holy Spirit. Using a different forum, she writes to express what was in her heart.

Now she fills purposely called and accepts this calling by taking captive her thoughts. First, giving it to Christ and asking His blessings, then by being obedient through the writing of this book, a composition of emotions, thoughts, and personal experiences over time.